Two Hal and Four Quarters

Brad and his big sister, Kristy,
were making some sandwiches
for their lunch.

"My sandwich is a square," said Kristy.
"It has four sides and four corners."

"My sandwich is a square, too," said Brad.
"I'm going to cut it in half."

"I've made two smaller sandwiches,"
said Brad.
"But they are not squares.
They are rectangles."

Kristy said, "Now I'm going to cut my big sandwich in half.
But I'm not going to make two rectangles.
I'm going to make two triangles."

She started cutting at one of the corners of her sandwich.

Kristy cut all the way across her sandwich.

"You have made two triangles," said Brad.
"They have three sides and three corners."

"I will cut them in half again," said Kristy.
"Then I'll have four little triangles."

"I've cut my big square sandwich into quarters," said Kristy.

"Now I have four little triangles."

"I've made quarters, too," said Brad.

"I've cut my rectangles in half.

Now I have four little squares."

"We can have this apple with our lunch," said Kristy.

"I'll cut it in half."

"An apple is like a ball," said Brad.

"So half an apple will be like half a ball."

"Yes, you are right," said Kristy.

"I can see a circle on my half
of the apple," said Brad.
"And I can see a circle
on your half, too."

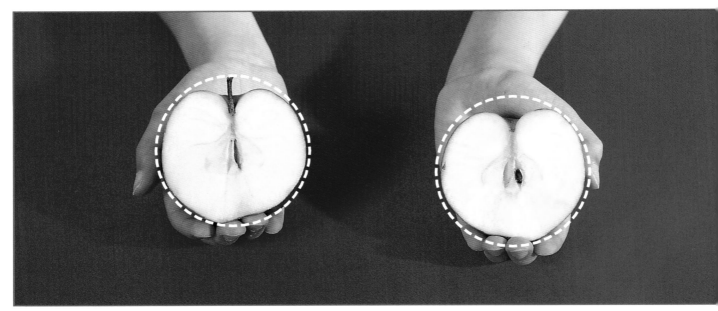

"Look, Kristy! My half and your half make a whole apple again," said Brad.

"Yes, they do," said Kristy.
"Now, let's eat our lunch!"

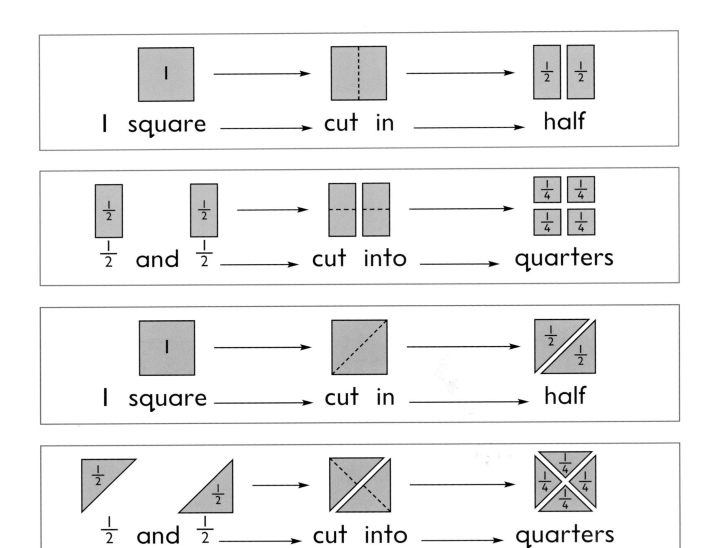

1 square   →   cut in   →   half

½ and ½   →   cut into   →   quarters

1 square   →   cut in   →   half

½ and ½   →   cut into   →   quarters